COMPARING ANIMAL TRAITS

KING COBRAS

HOODED VENOMOUS REPTILES

REBECCA E. HIRSCH

Lerner Publications ◆ Minneapolis

Lerner Publications Company
A division of Lerner Publishing Group, Inc.
241 First Avenue North
Minneapolis, MN 55401 USA

For reading levels and more information, look up this title at www.lernerbooks.com.

Photo Acknowledgments

The images in this book are used with the permission of: Dorling Kindersley Universal Images Group/ Newscom, p. 1; © John Terence Turner/Alamy, p. 4; © Hoberman Collection/Universal Images Group/Getty Images, p. 5; Mark O'Shea/NHPA/Photoshot/Newscom, p. 6; © Sanjeev Gupta/EPA/CORBIS, p. 7; © Michal Cerny/Alamy, p. 8; © Joe McDonald/CORBIS, p. 8 (left); © Dinodia Photos/Alamy, p. 9 (right); © iStockphoto .com/twildlife, p. 10; © Matt Jeppson/Shutterstock.com, p. 11 (top); © Mendez, Raymond/Animals Animals, p. 11 (bottom); © Laura Westlund/Independent Picture Service, p. 12; © Sandesh Kadur/naturepl.com, pp. 13, 24, 25 (all), 26; © E.R. Degginger/Alamy, p. 13; © iStockphoto.com/LeafenLin, p. 14; © iStockphoto .com/kosobu, p. 15; © iStockphoto.com/fremme, p. 16; © Biosphoto/SuperStock, p. 17 (left); © John Cancalosi/Alamy, p. 17 (right); © Indiapicture/Alamy, p. 18; © Michael Dick/Earth Scenes/Animals Animals, p. 19 (top); © Omar Ariff/iStock/Thinkstock, p. 19 (bottom); © blickwinkel/Alamy, p. 20; © Vincent Grafhorst/Minden Pictures/CORBIS, p. 21; © iStockphoto.com/mcswin, p. 22; © Patrick Aventurier/Getty Images, p. 23 (left); © iStockphoto.com/Paula Jones, p. 23 (right); © John Cancalosi/naturepl.com, p. 26; Jens Ressing//Deutsche Presse-AgenturNewscom, p. 27 (left); J. Lanki/Finland Tropicario/Wikimedia Commons (CC 3.0), p. 27 (right); © iStockphoto.com/Hawaiian, p. 28; © Lauren Hogan/National Geographic Society/ CORBIS, p. 29 (top); © Michael Kern/Visuals Unlimited/CORBIS, p. 29 (bottom).

Front cover: © Danita Delimont/Alamy.
Back cover: © Hoberman Collection/Universal Images Group/Getty Images.

Main body text set in Calvert MT Std 12/18. Typeface provided by Monotype Typography.

Library of Congress Cataloging-in-Publication Data

Hirsch, Rebecca E.
    King cobras : hooded venomous reptiles / Rebecca E. Hirsch.
        pages cm. – (Comparing animal traits)
    Includes bibliographical references.
    Audience: Ages 7–10.
    Audience: Grades K to grade 3.
    ISBN 978-1-4677-7983-8 (lb : alk. paper) — ISBN 978-1-4677-8280-7 (pb : alk. paper) —
ISBN 978-1-4677-8281-4 (EB pdf)
    1. King cobra—Juvenile literature. I. Title.
    QL666.O64H57 2015
    597.96'42—dc23
                                                                        2015000429

Manufactured in the United States of America
1 — BP —7/15/15

TABLE OF CONTENTS

MEET THE KING COBRA

A king cobra slithers over the ground and flicks its forked tongue. It smells a rat snake nearby. As the king cobra crawls closer to the rat snake, the cobra raises its head and prepares to strike.

King cobras belong to a group of animals called reptiles. Other animal groups you may know are mammals, amphibians, birds, fish, and insects. What makes reptiles different from these animal groups? All reptiles have three things in common. They are vertebrates, or animals with backbones. Reptiles have scaly skin.

A king cobra opens its mouth to strike.

And reptiles are cold-blooded. That means the temperature of the air or water around them warms or cools their bodies. King cobras share these traits with other reptiles. But king cobras are also unique. They have many traits that set them apart.

CHAPTER 1

WHAT DO KING COBRAS LOOK LIKE?

King cobras have long, slender bodies and no arms or legs.
Most adult king cobras are about 13 feet (4 meters) long and
weigh 15 to 20 pounds (6.8 to 9.1 kilograms). A king cobra's
body is covered with scales that are tough, like fingernails.
The scales protect the snake as it slithers over rocks and tree
branches. The king cobra's scaly skin comes in different colors.
A cobra may be light green, tan, or black. It may be solid in
color or have white or yellow stripes.

DID YOU KNOW?
King cobras can
be 18 feet (5.5 m)
long or more. That
makes them the
LONGEST
venomous snakes in
the world!

A king cobra has a flat head, a forked tongue, and stretchy jaws with two curved fangs. King cobras use their fangs to shoot venom into their prey. When threatened and unable to escape, a king cobra spreads its neck to form a hood and raises its head 3 to 6 feet (0.9 to 1.8 m) off the ground. This can put the cobra eye to eye with a full-grown person. The pose makes the snake look bigger and may scare away its enemy.

KING COBRAS VS. INDIAN COBRAS

An Indian cobra stands tall. It smells the air with its forked tongue and spreads its hood. Indian cobras live in deserts and mountains in Asia. These snakes can reach up to 8 feet (2.4 m) long, although most Indian cobra adults are about 5 feet (1.5 m) long. Indian cobras and king cobras look alike in many ways.

King cobras and Indian cobras both come in varied colors. An Indian cobra's skin can be black, gray, or brown. It may be solid in color or have white stripes or blotches.

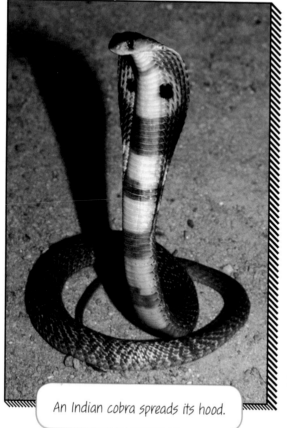

An Indian cobra spreads its hood.

Like a king cobra, an Indian cobra has two curved fangs for shooting venom and stretchy jaws that can open wide to swallow prey. To defend itself, it can raise its head and spread its neck to form a hood. Some Indian cobras have two spots connected by a curved line on the back of the hood. This pattern looks like large eyes and may help confuse its enemies.

COMPARE IT!

KING COBRA

VS.

INDIAN COBRA

13 FEET
(4 M)

TYPICAL
ADULT
LENGTH

5 FEET
(1.5 M)

SHARP, CURVED, SHOOT VENOM

◄ FANGS ►

SHARP, CURVED, SHOOT VENOM

Stands tall, spreads hood

DEFENSIVE
POSE

Stands tall, spreads hood

KING COBRAS VS. TEXAS HORNED LIZARDS

A Texas horned lizard shoots out its sticky, pink tongue and catches a large ant. Texas horned lizards live in deserts in southwestern North America. These spiky reptiles can grow to 4 to 6 inches (10 to 15 centimeters) from the head to the base of the tail. They look quite different from king cobras.

King cobras have long, thin bodies, but the bodies of Texas horned lizards are wide and flat. King cobras have smooth, striped skin. Texas horned lizards have pebble-shaped spots on their skin. These lizards are also covered with spiny scales. Together the spines and the spots camouflage the lizards against the rocky ground.

Texas horned lizards have rough, spiny skin.

King cobras have forked tongues and sharp, curved fangs. Texas horned lizards have long, sticky tongues and blunt teeth that are shaped like pegs. They use their tongues and teeth to catch and chew ants.

DID YOU KNOW?

A Texas horned lizard defends itself by squirting a jet of **BLOOD** from its eyes. The blood surprises the attacker and may allow the horned lizard to escape.

CHAPTER 2

WHERE DO KING COBRAS LIVE?

King cobras slither through the grass in southern Asia. You can find them in many different habitats. King cobras might inhabit rain forests, grasslands, swamps, or farm fields. A king cobra's skin helps it blend into its surroundings. King cobras

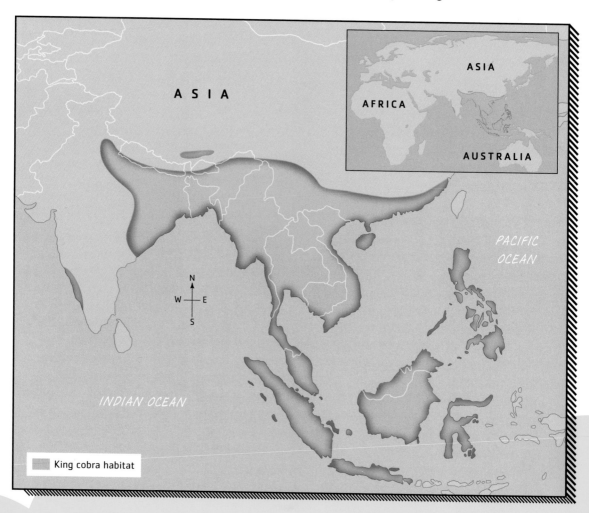

King cobra habitat

that live in dark forests have dark skin. King cobras in sunnier habitats have lighter skin. As they move through their habitat, they can be hard to spot.

King cobras live near lakes, rivers, and streams. They inhabit places with dense brush, fallen logs, or other good hiding spots. A king cobra spends time out in the open, basking in the sun to warm its body. By having a hiding spot nearby, it can quickly escape any danger.

King cobras blend in with their surroundings.

King cobras move through their habitat in search of prey. They hunt on land, in trees, and in water. Other snakes are their most common meal. They also eat eggs and small animals such as lizards and rodents.

DID YOU KNOW?
The **MONGOOSE** is the king cobra's main predator. This quick mammal bites the cobra's neck before the snake can attack.

KING COBRAS VS. WATER MONITORS

A water monitor crawls across a riverbank, dragging its long tail. It slips into the river and uses its tail to swim along the surface. Water monitors have black or brown skin with yellow spots. They usually grow to about 5 feet (1.5 m) long. These large lizards and king cobras live in similar habitats.

As with king cobras, water monitors live in many different

habitats across southern Asia. They live in swamps, rain forests, grasslands, and farm fields. Like king cobras, water monitors are carnivores. They will eat almost any animal. They eat insects, spiders, fish, birds, bird eggs, rodents, monkeys, snakes, turtles, young crocodiles, and even other monitor lizards. They also scavenge garbage and dead animals.

Water monitors are good swimmers.

Much like king cobras, water monitors live near water. They often get from place to place by swimming, but they can also be found on land or in trees. When water monitors rest, they hide in trees, under bushes or fallen trees, or in a burrow in a riverbank.

KING COBRAS VS. CHUCKWALLAS

A chuckwalla suns itself on a rock. When it spies a hawk flying overhead, it slips into a crack in the rock to stay safe. Chuckwallas are large, bulky lizards that can grow to 16 inches (41 cm) long, including their long tails. Chuckwallas and king cobras are found in different habitats. King cobras live in tropical habitats in southern Asia. Chuckwallas live in rocky deserts in southwestern North America.

King cobras are carnivores. But chuckwallas are mostly herbivores. They live on desert flowers, fruits, and leaves. They also sometimes eat insects. A chuckwalla's most common meal is the fruit of the prickly pear cactus, which is plentiful in its desert habitat.

Chuckwallas bask in the hot desert sun.

King cobras live near water, but chuckwallas don't need water in their habitat. They get water from the plants they eat. But chuckwallas do need rocks. When frightened, they hide in cracks in the rocks and puff up their bodies with air. This wedges chuckwallas in the rocks and makes it difficult for predators to remove them.

COMPARE IT!

KING COBRAS

VS.

CHUCKWALLAS

SOUTHERN ASIA ◀ WHERE IT LIVES ▶ **SOUTHWESTERN NORTH AMERICA**

RAIN FORESTS, SWAMPS, GRASSLANDS, FARM FIELDS ◀ HABITAT ▶ **DESERTS**

Snakes, lizards, eggs, small mammals ◀ FOOD ▶ Flowers, fruit, leaves, some insects

CHAPTER 3

KING COBRAS IN ACTION

A king cobra hunts alone. It slithers through its habitat, searching for snakes to eat. A king cobra tracks its prey with a flick of its forked tongue. The tongue picks up smells from the air. The cobra touches the tip of its tongue to an organ on the top of its mouth, called the Jacobson's organ, which senses the smell.

King cobras use their tongues to smell.

When a king cobra draws close to its prey, the cobra strikes. With a quick bite, it injects venom into the animal with its fangs. The venom stops the prey's breathing and heartbeat. A king cobra eats its prey by opening its stretchy jaws wide. Inch by inch, a king cobra swallows its dinner whole.

A king cobra swallows a snake.

King cobras can be dangerous to humans. These powerful reptiles usually flee from people, but if cornered, they will fight. First, a king cobra spreads its hood, makes a hiss that sounds like a growling dog, and raises its head high off the ground. This is a warning. If the person doesn't retreat, the snake may attack. A bite from a king cobra can be deadly if not treated quickly.

DID YOU KNOW?

A king cobra can inject a large quantity of deadly **VENOM** in a single bite. One bite can inject enough venom to kill an elephant.

KING COBRAS VS. BLACK MAMBAS

A black mamba slithers over the ground. It flicks its tongue to smell the air for prey. Black mambas live in eastern and southern Africa. These snakes can grow up to 14 feet (4.3 m) long and are named for the black color of the inside of their mouths. Black mambas and king cobras are both predators, and they hunt in similar ways.

King cobras and black mambas hunt by chasing their prey. A black mamba tracks down small mammals and birds by smelling the air with its tongue. Once a black mamba is near its prey, it kills with a quick bite from its venomous fangs.

DID YOU KNOW?

A black mamba is one of the **FASTEST** snakes in the world. It can slither up to 12 miles (20 kilometers) per hour. That's faster than the jogging speed of a human.

Both king cobras and black mambas will flee from danger but will fight if trapped. As a warning, a black mamba raises its head and neck and spreads its narrow hood. It opens its black mouth and hisses. If the enemy does not retreat, the black mamba strikes with its deadly bite.

KING COBRAS VS. MARINE IGUANAS

A marine iguana climbs over wet rocks along the shore. It tears algae off the rocks with its sharp teeth. Marine iguanas live in the Galápagos Islands near the western coast of South America. This reptile has a crest of spines along its back and long claws on its feet. A marine iguana can grow to 5 feet (1.5 m) long.

Marine iguanas behave differently than king cobras. King cobras are hunters, but marine iguanas eat only plants. King cobras hunt alone, but marine iguanas live in groups. Together marine iguanas forage for algae along the shore and in the water. King cobras have a deadly bite, but marine iguanas do not. They use their sharp teeth to tear algae. They will bite in self-defense, but they don't have any venom.

Marine iguanas eat the algae that grows on wet rocks.

COMPARE IT!

KING COBRAS

VS.

MARINE IGUANAS

HUNTS ALONE ◄ HOW IT FINDS FOOD ► **FORAGES IN GROUPS**

SNAKES ◄ MOST COMMON FOOD ► **ALGAE**

Venomous ◄ BITE ► Nonvenomous

CHAPTER 4

THE LIFE CYCLE OF KING COBRAS

A king cobra is the only snake in the world that builds a nest for its eggs. After mating, a female uses her body to push together leaves to build a nest. She lays twenty to fifty eggs in the nest. Then she covers the eggs with more leaves. As the leaves in the nest rot, they give off heat that keeps the eggs warm. The mother cobra wraps herself around the nest to protect it. The eggs are ready to hatch in two to three months. Just before the eggs hatch, the mother slithers away. The cobra hatchlings are on their own.

Each baby snake is 15 to 20 inches (38 to 51 cm) long and half an inch (1.3 cm) wide. That's about the size of a shoelace. A baby's venom is as deadly as an adult's. As the young cobras grow, a new layer of skin grows beneath the skin that is visible. Then the old outer layer splits, and the snakes slither out. King cobras continue to grow new skin and shed old skin throughout their lives.

Leaves protect and warm the eggs in a king cobra nest.

These young king cobras are leaving their shells.

In five or six years, king cobras are ready to mate and have offspring of their own. With traits they have inherited from their parents, such as scaly skin and venomous fangs, they can survive for about twenty years in the wild.

DID YOU KNOW?
Male king cobras **FIGHT** each other for mates. They don't bite—they neck wrestle. Two males raise their bodies, twine together, and try to push each other to the ground.

KING COBRAS VS. AFRICAN ROCK PYTHONS

An African rock python rests between two rocks. This large snake lives in Africa, south of the Sahara. The python has a thick body with patterned skin, and it can grow up to 20 feet (6.1 m) long. African rock pythons and king cobras have similar life cycles.

As with king cobras, African rock pythons lay eggs. A female python lays twenty to one hundred eggs in a tree hollow, a termite mound, or an empty animal burrow. She does not build a nest as a king cobra does. But like a king cobra, the rock python wraps herself around the eggs to protect them.

An African rock python slithers between rocks.

In two to three months, the python eggs hatch. The python hatchlings are able to take care of themselves right away, just like baby king cobras. African rock pythons grow up in three to five years, compared to five or six years for king cobras. Pythons may live for thirty years, which is longer than a king cobra's life span.

COMPARE IT!

KING COBRAS

VS.

AFRICAN ROCK PYTHONS

20 TO 50 ◀ NUMBER OF EGGS ▶ **20 TO 100**

Guards and protects eggs

◀ HOW MOTHER CARES FOR YOUNG ▶

Guards and protects eggs

20 YEARS ◀ LIFE SPAN ▶ **30 YEARS**

KING COBRAS VS. JACKSON'S CHAMELEONS

Jackson's chameleons climb trees in eastern Africa. These color-changing reptiles can grow up to 13.5 inches (34 cm) long. Males have three horns on their heads. Jackson's chameleons and king cobras look different, and they have different life cycles.

Unlike female king cobras, female Jackson's chameleons give birth to live young. Between eight and thirty young chameleons grow in soft-shelled eggs inside the mother's body for six to seven months. Then the mother chameleon delivers one soft, sticky egg at a time onto a tree branch. After a short rest, the young chameleon breaks out of the soft shell. The chameleon mother leaves her young to fend for themselves. A baby chameleon is about 2 inches (5.1 cm) long, much smaller than a baby king cobra.

A Jackson's chameleon perches on a branch.

The horns of this young Jackson's chameleon are still small.

Jackson's chameleons grow up faster than king cobras. King cobras take five or six years to reach adulthood, but Jackson's chameleons are grown in just nine or ten months. They have shorter lives than king cobras too. Jackson's chameleons live for just eight years, less than half the life span of a king cobra.

DID YOU KNOW?

Male Jackson's chameleons sometimes FIGHT during mating season. They puff up with air to look bigger, turn brilliant colors, and try to poke each other with their horns.

KING COBRAS TRAIT CHART

This book explores the ways king cobras are similar to and different from other reptiles. What other reptiles would you like to learn about?

	COLD-BLOODED	SCALES ON BODY	LAY EGGS	HOODED HEAD AND NECK	CARNIVORE	VENOMOUS
KING COBRA	X	X	X	X	X	X
INDIAN COBRA	X	X	X	X	X	X
TEXAS HORNED LIZARD	X	X	X		X	
WATER MONITOR	X	X	X		X	
CHUCKWALLA	X	X	X			
BLACK MAMBA	X	X	X	X	X	X
MARINE IGUANA	X	X	X			
AFRICAN ROCK PYTHON	X	X	X		X	
JACKSON'S CHAMELEON	X	X			X	

algae: a plant or plantlike organism (such as seaweed) that mostly grows in water

basking: lying or resting in a warm place

burrow: a hole in the ground made by an animal for shelter or protection

camouflage: to hide or disguise an animal

carnivores: meat-eating animals

forage: to search for food

habitats: environments where animals naturally live. A habitat is the place where an animal can find food, water, air, shelter, and a place to raise its young.

hatchlings: young animals that have recently hatched from eggs

herbivores: plant-eating animals

predators: animals that hunt other animals for food

prey: an animal that is hunted and killed by a predator for food

scavenge: to feed on dead or decaying animals

traits: features that are inherited from parents. Body size and skin color are examples of inherited traits.

venom: poison produced by some snakes and passed to a victim by biting

LERNER

SOURCE

Expand learning beyond the printed book. Download free, complementary educational resources for this book from our website, www.lernerresource.com.

SELECTED BIBLIOGRAPHY

"Animals." *National Geographic*. Accessed September 8, 2014. http://animals.nationalgeographic.com/animals/.

Areste, Manuel, and Rafael Cebrian. *Snakes of the World*. New York: Sterling, 2003.

"San Diego Zoo Animals." San Diego Zoo. Accessed September 8, 2014. http://animals.sandiegozoo.org/animals/.

Young, Diana. "*Ophiophagus hannah*: Hamadryad, King Cobra." *Animal Diversity Web*. Last modified June 7, 1999. http://animaldiversity.org/accounts/Ophiophagus_hannah/.

FURTHER INFORMATION

Doeden, Matt. *Deadly Venomous Animals*. Minneapolis: Lerner Publications, 2013. Open this book to learn more about king cobras and other deadly animals that use venom.

National Geographic—King Cobra vs. Olive Water Snake
http://video.nationalgeographic.com/video/king-cobra-vs-water-snake-predation
Watch a baby king cobra hunt and catch an olive water snake.

San Diego Zoo—Cobra
http://animals.sandiegozoo.org/animals/cobra
You can see photos and learn more facts about king cobras and other kinds of cobras.

Woodward, John. *Everything You Need to Know about Snakes*. New York: DK, 2013. Learn about snakes from all around the world.

INDEX